The Smart & Easy Guide To Mortgages & Home Financing: How To Finance Real Estate To Make The House Buying Process Successful

Mark Dennison

Legal Stuff

Copyright Information

Copyright © 2013 Checkmate Marketing Group LLC. All rights reserved worldwide.

No part of this publication may be replicated, redistributed, or given away in any form without the prior written consent of the publisher.

Checkmate Marketing Group LLC

Earnings Disclaimer

EVERY EFFORT HAS BEEN MADE TO ACCURATELY REPRESENT THIS PRODUCT AND IT'S POTENTIAL. IN TERMS OF EARNINGS, THERE IS NO GUARANTEE THAT YOU WILL EARN ANY MONEY USING THE TECHNIQUES AND IDEAS IN THIS MATERIAL. INFORMATION PRESENTED ON THIS BOOK IS NOT TO BE INTERPRETED AS A PROMISE OR GUARANTEE OF EARNINGS. EARNING POTENTIAL IS ENTIRELY DEPENDENT ON THE PERSON USING OUR PRODUCT, IDEAS AND TECHNIQUES.

ANY CLAIMS MADE OF ACTUAL EARNINGS OR EXAMPLES OF ACTUAL RESULTS CAN BE VERIFIED UPON REQUEST. YOUR LEVEL OF SUCCESS IN ATTAINING THE RESULTS CLAIMED IN OUR MATERIALS DEPENDS ON THE TIME YOU DEVOTE TO THE PROGRAM, IDEAS AND TECHNIQUES MENTIONED, YOUR FINANCES, KNOWLEDGE AND VARIOUS SKILLS. SINCE THESE FACTORS DIFFER ACCORDING TO INDIVIDUALS, WE CANNOT GUARANTEE YOUR SUCCESS OR INCOME LEVEL.

ANY AND ALL FORWARD LOOKING STATEMENTS HERE OR ON ANY OF OUR SALES MATERIAL ARE INTENDED TO EXPRESS OUR OPINION OF EARNINGS POTENTIAL. MANY FACTORS WILL BE IMPORTANT IN DETERMINING YOUR ACTUAL RESULTS AND NO GUARANTEES ARE MADE THAT YOU WILL ACHIEVE RESULTS SIMILAR TO OURS OR ANYONE ELSES. NO GUARANTEES ARE MADE THAT YOU WILL ACHIEVE ANY RESULTS FROM OUR IDEAS AND TECHNIQUES IN OUR MATERIAL.

Limitation of Liability

THE MATERIALS IN THIS BOOK ARE PROVIDED "AS IS" WITHOUT ANY EXPRESS OR IMPLIED WARRANTY OF ANY KIND INCLUDING WARRANTIES OF MERCHANTABILITY, NONINFRINGEMENT OF INTELLECTUAL PROPERTY, OR FITNESS FOR ANY PARTICULAR PURPOSE. IN NO EVENT SHALL OR ITS AGENTS OR OFFICERS BE LIABLE FOR ANY DAMAGES WHATSOEVER (INCLUDING, WITHOUT LIMITATION, DAMAGES FOR LOSS OF PROFITS, BUSINESS INTERRUPTION, LOSS OF INFORMATION, INJURY OR DEATH) ARISING OUT OF THE USE OF OR INABILITY TO USE THE MATERIALS, EVEN IF HAS BEEN ADVISED OF THE POSSIBILITY OF SUCH LOSS OR DAMAGES.

Table of Contents

Mortgage Loan Basics 6
Advantages of Using a Mortgage Broker 11
Mortgage Mysteries Unraveled 15
Types of Mortgages 16
    Special Loans: 16
    Convertible Loans: 16
    Fixed Rate Loans: 18
Fees 19
Other Need-to-Know Terms 20
Government Mortgages – The Need-to-Know About VA and FHA Mortgages 22
Mortgages and Your Credit Score 26
Questions You Should Ask Before Signing Your Name on the Dotted Line 29
Shopping Around for the Best Mortgage Interest Rates 33
Learn to Negotiate Mortgage Points 36
Going Through Mortgage Paperwork with a Fine Tooth Comb 40
Closing Costs and Fees Need-to-Knows 44
Advantages and Disadvantages of Balloon Payment Mortgages 49
What Are Bridge Loans? 53
What Does Home Refinancing Entail? 57
Shopping for the Best Second Mortgage Terms 60
Reasons Your Mortgage Loan Has Been Denied 63
Should You Repay Your Mortgage Loan Early or Not? 66
The Fundamentals of PMI (Private Mortgage Insurance) 70
Is Home Equity Refinancing Right for You? 74
We Want Your Feedback on This Book! 76

Mortgage Loan Basics

Everyone isn't fortunate enough to have the money needed to purchase a house sitting in his bank account. Therefore, if you're the typical home seeker, you're going to need a mortgage loan.

Many types of mortgage loans exist; however, there are two main categories that all types of mortgage loans fall under. These are governmental and conventional loans. From either of these categories, mortgages can be further grouped as adjustable rate loans, fixed rate loans, or any combination of the two.

There are three government departments from which the U.S. government offers mortgages. They are:

1. The RHS (Rural Housing Service) of the U.S. Department of Agriculture.

2. The HUD (U.S. Department of Housing and Urban Development).

3. The VA (U.S. Department of Veterans' Affairs)

Apart from these three government department mortgages, various counties, states and cities provide other reasonably priced housing plans. These plans are usually fixed rate mortgages with very low interest rates.

All non-governmental mortgages are referred to as conventional mortgages. These types of mortgages fall under two main categories – non-conforming and conforming mortgage loans.

Conforming mortgage loans are based on conditions and guidelines set by the Freddie Mac and Fannie Mae companies. These companies contact lending institutions, buy mortgage loans from them, bundle them into various securities and then sell them to investors.

Freddie Mac and Fannie Mae both set the ground rules for income requirements, borrowers' credit, loan amounts, acceptable properties and down payments on all conforming mortgage loans. Additionally, each year, both companies make publicly known the loan limits for individuals applying for their first mortgage loan. These rates can be found on the companies' websites – www.freddiemac.com and www.fanniemae.com.

Non-conforming loans can be classified as either B/C loans or jumbo loans. B/C mortgage loans are reserved for individuals who have a history of late payments. Also, they are given to those individuals who have previously received mortgage loans, but have filed for bankruptcy or foreclosure.

On the other hand, jumbo mortgage loans are those loans whose rates are higher than the maximal rates issued by Fannie Mae and Freddie Mac. Due to the fact that jumbo loans are purchased at a lower degree, they have much higher interest rates than conforming mortgage loans.

Earlier, it was mentioned that both governmental and conventional mortgage loans can be grouped as either adjustable rate or fixed rate mortgages. Have a closer look at what these terms actually mean.

An adjustable rate mortgage gives you the flexibility of changing your monthly payments from time to time. The interest of adjustable rate mortgages is dependent on the index that is applied to the interest rate. These indexes are inclusive of:

- Fannie Mae's RNY (Required Net Yeild)

- LIBOR – London Inter-Bank Offering Rates

- 11th District COFI (Cost of Funds Index)

- T-Bill – (Treasury Bill)

- CODI – Certificate of Deposit Index

- COSI – Cost of Savings Index

- 12 MTA (Month Treasury Average)

- Prime Rate

- CMT – Constant Maturity Treasury

Per contra, with a fixed mortgage loan, the monthly payments remain the same until the end of the loan. The payment period for these mortgage loans generally range from 10 to 30 years; however, you'll find that the payment period for the most in-demand mortgage loans range from 15 to 30 years. Keep in mind that you'll pay less interest the shorter your payment period is.

One of the best places for you to access information about mortgage loans is the Internet. As such, there are several mortgage companies that offer their potential and existing clients various services and resources through this medium.

But before you rush to choose the mortgage loan that you think will work best for you, there are some factors that you need to take into consideration based on your financial status. These factors include:

- How much can you afford to pay monthly on your mortgage?

- Is the down payment affordable?

- What's the payment period you're considering?

- Do you plan on making additional principal payments?

- Do you have a stable income?

Advantages of Using a Mortgage Broker

Whether you're upgrading your home or you're seeking to purchase your first house, you're most likely going to need a mortgage loan to assist you with the payments.

But where is the best place for you to get a mortgage loan? Is it better to use a mortgage broker or a bank? There are quite a few factors that you need to consider when making this decision; however, it will all come down to your personal preference.

Another question that you'll find yourself asking is, *"what's the difference between a loan officer and a mortgage broker?"* The difference between these two is quite simple.

A loan officer is employed by a lending company to process mortgages and loans. On the other hand, a mortgage broker is an independent agent. Additionally, a loan officer is restricted to working at one lending company, while a mortgage broker is free to work with any amount of lending companies that he chooses to.

There are several types of mortgages that a loan officer will be able to offer you; however, these all come from a single lending company. A mortgage broker, on the other hand, works with a varied number of lending companies in order to get mortgage terms and interest rates that are most suitable for your needs.

A mortgage broker is paid to bring lenders and borrowers together, and is essentially the "*go-between.*" They can't lend you the money needed to purchase your home, but they will find the lending company that will be able to do so.

Research is an imperative part of a mortgage broker's job. His job is to assess you as a homebuyer, take your credit score into consideration, and find the lending company that will be most suitable for your mortgage needs.

Once the mortgage broker locates the best lender and gets the go-ahead from you, he will submit your loan application and work with both you and the lender until the loan is granted.

If you have the time to dedicate to the loan process, you can always complete the necessary research on your own. However, it's best to use a mortgage broker as he already has business relationships with these lending companies, and can work with them to find the best deals for you.

Whether mortgage brokers are based online or in a traditional brick-and-mortar office, they all have business relationships with lending agencies across the country. However, using a lending company outside of your state does have its advantages and disadvantages.

For instance, getting a mortgage loan from an out-of-state lending company may get you better interest rates; on the other hand, that company might be clueless as it relates to properties in your area.

But this will probably not have an effect on your mortgage. The only issue you may face with an out-of-state lending company is an application processing delay. This delay often times happens when the company is waiting to ensure that all the questions and terms regarding the property are answered and accurate.

Are you worried that you may not be able to purchase your dream home because you can't secure a bank loan? Once mortgage brokers are around, there's no need for you to worry.

They are particularly known to find lending companies to accept applications that were refused by banks. If a bank has recently denied your application for a mortgage, you shouldn't delay in making an appointment to talk to a mortgage broker.

In order to save time and to prevent hassles, you should bring copies of your credit history to your initial meeting with a mortgage broker. By reviewing your credit history, he will have a better idea of the type and terms of the mortgage loan that will be best suited for you.

There are two things that you ought to bear in mind when thinking about using a bank or a mortgage broker. These are:

1. There's a transaction fee that is paid to the mortgage broker; as such, he's working towards your best interests as well as his.

2. Mortgage needs differ from person to person. With that being said, you need to complete your own research before deciding whether to use a bank or mortgage broker. Talk to friends and relatives, who are already homeowners, as well as to your real estate agent.

Mortgage Mysteries Unraveled

When you initially start looking at mortgages, you may feel overwhelmed by all the options that are available. At first glance, seeing the various types of forms, fees, regulations and terms may confuse you, particularly when you have no prior knowledge about mortgages.

But once you learn the fundamentals of mortgages, you'll realize that it's not that difficult to apply for a loan to purchase your dream home. Take a look at some of the fundamentals of mortgages that you should know prior to applying for a loan.

Types of Mortgages

Although there are a variety of mortgage loans available, the three primary ones are special, convertible and fixed rate loans.

Special Loans:

- **Veteran Affairs (VA) Mortgage Loans** – These mortgage loans are given to veterans of the armed forces or their surviving spouses (if spouses remarry they are no longer eligible to receive these loans).

- **FHA (Federal Housing Administration) Mortgage Loans** – FHA loans are primarily designed for Americans who are on the lower end of the income spectrum.

Convertible Loans:

- **Buydown Mortgages** – Persons looking for lower monthly payments and interest rates generally opt for these loans.

- **Reverse Mortgages** – These mortgage loans are for seniors (must be 62 years and older), and allow homeowners to borrow against their homes. No mortgage repayment is required until the sale of the house, or the death of the borrower.

- **Balloon Payment Mortgages** – With balloon mortgages, the mortgage isn't completely amortized; as such, a lump sum is due at the time of maturity.

- **Interest-Only Mortgages** – If you choose this type of convertible mortgage, your monthly payments will only be the interest rates that have accumulated from the borrowed principal. However, you'll be required to repay the principal amount at some point in time.

- **Hybrid ARMs (Adjustable Rate Mortgages)** – These mortgages are blends of the traits of a fixed rate and an adjustable rate mortgage. Initially, there'll be a period of a fixed interest rate, after which the period of adjustable rate will follow.

- **Convertible ARMs (Adjustable Rate Mortgages)** – Convertible ARMs give you the option of converting from an adjustable rate mortgage to a fixed rate. Keep in mind that there are charges that apply to making this switch.

Fixed Rate Loans:

The most popular types of fixed rate mortgages are:

- **Bi-weekly Repayment** – Repayments are required every two weeks.

- **15-year Repayment** – Fixed repayments are required monthly for 15 years.

- **30-year Repayment** – Fixed repayments are required monthly for 30 years.

Fees

When applying for a mortgage loan, it's essential that you pay specific fees. These fees are inclusive of:

- **Organizational Fees** – Needed to pay the lending company for the processing of the application.

- **Down Payment** – This is the deposit that you'll have to put down for the purchase of your home. Generally, the down payment falls between one and 20 percent.

- **Closing Costs** – You'll have to pay for transference of home ownership. These costs vary, and are usually between one and three percent of the total of your loan.

- **Appraisal Fees** – This fee is paid to an appraiser to evaluate the value of the home you wish to purchase.

Other Need-to-Know Terms

The field of mortgages is packed with several need-to-know terms. Listed below are just a few of them.

- **Escrow** – The place where a third party keeps all sensitive information and money passed between you and the lender, until the transaction has been completed.

- **PITI** (pronounced "*pity*") – An acronym that identifies the parts of a mortgage payment. Your mortgage payment will be a sum of the **P**rinciple (your loan amount), **I**nterest, **T**axes and **I**nsurance.

- **Pre-qualifying** – This basically means that you qualify for a mortgage loan before you apply for one. Pre-qualifying also helps you to have an idea of the loan amount you can afford, based on your budget.

- **Truth In Lending Disclosure** – A form that allows you to know your complete loan cost in a dollar and percentage outline.

- **Loan Locks** – Loan locks help you to secure a set interest rate at the initial part of the mortgage application process. Without a loan lock, the lender can decrease or increase the interest rate without you having a say.

- **GFE (Good Faith Estimate)** – Is given to you by the mortgage broker or lender, and provides you with an estimate of the charges of the settlement and the loan terms that will apply if your loan is approved.

- **Mortgage Points** – Also referred to as "*discount points*" or "*origination points*," this up-front payment enables you to reduce the loan's interest rate, so that your monthly payments will be lower. Keep in mind that a single point is equivalent to one percent of the amount of the loan.

  The information listed above is just basic knowledge. There's a lot more information about mortgages available. However, this information will give you the push you need to start the loan application process. Whenever you need clarification or more details about mortgages, it's best to seek the advice of a lender or other financial professional.

Government Mortgages – The Need-to-Know About VA and FHA Mortgages

No matter what your financial situation is, you'll find that you can still qualify for a mortgage loan, particularly those that are funded by the government. Two such mortgage loans are the VA and FHA mortgages.

VA (Veterans Assistance) mortgages are specially designed for U.S. veterans, or their surviving spouses. Things that you need to know about VA mortgages include:

- The guaranteed amount that a veteran receives is referred to as an *"entitlement."*

- A majority of lending companies offer VA mortgages.

- Generally, VA mortgages don't require you to pay private mortgage insurance or a down payment.

- Due to the fact that monthly mortgage insurance doesn't apply to VA mortgages, you'll find that the monthly payments are quite lower than other mortgage loans.

- You can utilize these mortgage loans for refinancing.

- You'll be required to pay a funding fee (generally two percent of the loan amount) at the closing of the VA loan.

FHA (Federal Housing Administration) mortgage loans enable Americans in the lower income bracket to acquire money for purchasing a home. This loan can also be given to first-time home buyers. Initially, FHA loans started off as government loans; however, they have gradually been transferred to independent mortgage insurance companies.

Here's a look at some of the types of FHA loans:

- **Insured FHA Loans** – For this loan, mortgage insurance is required whether you are interested in refinancing or buying a home. Requirements for insured FHA loans include: health-related facilities, multi-family and single family properties and manufactured homes. You're guaranteed lower mortgage loan costs and down payments with this type of loan.

- **Adjustable Rate FHA Loans** – This type of FHA allows you to adjust (increase or decrease) the loan's interest rate over a given period.

- **Rising Income FHA Loans** – With this particular type of FHA, initially, your mortgage payments will be low. However, as time progresses and your income increases, the mortgage payments will also increase. Rising income FHA loans are best suited for first time home buyers and families that are just starting out.

- **Energy Efficient FHA Loans** – These loans enable you to save on your utility expenses, as you're given a loan to add energy efficient appliances to an existing or new home. By taking advantage of this loan, you're saving energy while cutting your loan cost. An energy consultant or a home energy rating system determines the loan cost to be cut.

- **Condominiums FHA Loans** – Not everyone is interested in purchasing a traditional home. If you fall into this category, you can get an FHA that offers you insurance to purchase a condominium. You can also get a loan for the upkeep of the condominium, but this is only if it will be your primary residence. In order to qualify for this loan, the area is required to have at most four units, and the condominiums can't be transformed from dated apartment buildings.

If you're looking to purchase or refinance a home and believe that your financial stability will prevent you from getting a regular mortgage loan, you can try applying for VA or FHA mortgage loans.

Mortgages and Your Credit Score

When thinking about purchasing a new home, persons generally try to secure a loan at the bank. However, as it relates to lending money, a majority of financial institutions prefer to lend money only to individuals with a good credit score.

If you have a bad credit score, you'll still be able to get a mortgage loan from some lending companies, but these loans (referred to as *"bad credit loans"*) come at a high price. The fees and the interest rates of bad credit loans are extremely high, and you just might end up paying more than the house's original price.

It's quite evident that your credit score does have an effect on your mortgage whether or not you get the loan, the type of mortgage you get and how much you'll have to repay. As such, it's advised that you review your FICO credit score prior to applying for a mortgage loan.

Five factors that influence your FICO credit score are:

1. **Payment History** – This is inclusive of any payment that was late or missed. It will also include the various types of monthly payments you make (e.g. credit card, house, car, etc.). Your payment history makes up for approximately 35 percent of your credit score. Therefore, if you have a good credit score, your payment history will most likely

show that you have a few or no missed payments, and constantly make your monthly payments on time.

2. **Amount Owed On Various Accounts** – If you regularly max out your credit cards or have high balances on a varied number of accounts; you're going to have a bad credit score. However, if you only have one or two accounts to which a balance is applied, then your credit score will most likely be good.

3. **Credit History Length** – The length of your credit history will assist lenders in knowing if you constantly pay your bills on time, and how well you're able to manage your finances. Keep in mind that you won't see an immediate credit score increase to a year old account that's managed perfectly; however, you'll definitely see an increase in your credit score if you continue to manage it well for the next few years.

4. **Credit Types** – Credit types refer to student loan or car payments, mortgages and credit cards. You'll have a low credit score if your most frequently used credit type overburdens high interest credit sources, like your credit card.

5. **Recent or New Credit History** – Newly or recently opened accounts will have an effect on your credit score. You can open new accounts or request new credit; however, if you do this frequently, your credit score will ultimately suffer.

If you don't have the best credit score but wish to apply for a mortgage loan, there are ways in which you can improve your score. You can start by requesting a copy of your credit report from TransUnion, Equifax or Experian. Legally, once per year you're entitled to a single free copy of your credit report; however, you'll have to pay for any additional copies.

Once you've received your credit report, review it and see which areas you need to improve. If you notice any discrepancies in your report (such as omissions or other types of errors), inform the credit bureau immediately. You'll be required to provide documentation.

Bear in mind that your payment history accounts for a big percentage of your credit score. As such, you should strive to never miss payments and constantly pay your bills on time.

Take advantage of automatic monthly payments, and refrain from frequently opening and closing accounts. Instead, you should try to increase your credit score by responsibly using the accounts you already have.

Questions You Should Ask Before Signing Your Name on the Dotted Line

One of the most important things you should remember about mortgage loans is to always ask questions prior to writing your name on the dotted line, particularly if you're unsure about the terms and conditions.

Don't shy away from asking your mortgage broker or lender questions, as the answers you receive have a great impact on choosing the most suitable mortgage loan for your needs.

- **How Long Does the Mortgage Loan Application Process Take?** – Generally, the application process takes approximately 45 to 60 days to be completed; however, there are times when mortgages are processed in just 30 days. The length of the application process is dependent on how quickly the lender verifies your bank accounts and employment history, and also how quickly they can obtain your credit report and have the property appraised.

- **What Documents are Needed for the Application Process**? – Different lenders will ask for different documents, but generally you'll be asked to present proof of your assets and income.

- **What are the Qualifications for a Home Mortgage Loan?** – Qualifications that will help you to acquire a home mortgage loan include: debts, assets, employment status, credit history and income.

- **What's the Minimum Down Payment Required?** – While some loans require as much as a 20 percent down payment, other loans require far less. You should work out your down payment first, and then you can go from there. Once your down payment is finalized, the lender can offer you a variety of loan terms and interest rates.

- **What's the Annual Mortgage Interest Required?** – The best way to compare mortgage loan rates from various lenders is to ask for and analyze their APR (Annual Percentage Rate) of the mortgage interest.

- **What Are Origination Fees?** – An origination fee is an upfront payment that acts as prepaid mortgage interest. These fees help to decrease the interest rate of your mortgage loan, and are generally paid at closing time using points.

- **Are Locked-In Mortgage Interest Rates Available?** Yes, they are. If your interest rate isn't locked-in, it will decrease or increase prior to your closing time. As such, it's advised that you opt for locked-in rates. Be sure to ask the lender about the lock-in fee, or if you can use your mortgage points to lock-in.

- **What's a Good Faith Estimate (GFE)?** – There's a long list of fees that goes along with applying for a mortgage loan. With that being said, your mortgage lender or broker is legally required to present you with a list of all the estimated closing costs, prior to you applying for the loan. Keep in mind that upfront payments are required for fees such as the loan application and property appraisal fees.

- **What is a Prepayment Penalty?** – This is a clause that appears in your mortgage contract which states that a penalty will apply if you repay your mortgage within a certain timeframe. Prior to signing your mortgage contract, ensure that you know and understand how the penalty will be calculated and the length of the penalty period.

- **Will There be Any Delays in the Home Mortgage Loan Application Process?** – It all depends on the accuracy and completeness of the information you provide the lender. As such, you should ensure that your application form is completed properly and that the information is authentic. You should notify your mortgage lender immediately if there are any sudden changes to your financial or personal status. This applies to changes in marital, income or employment statuses.

Shopping Around for the Best Mortgage Interest Rates

Lately, mortgage interest rates have fallen to an all-time low; as such, more people are now able to purchase homes. It has never been so easy to shop around for the best mortgage interest rates, now that the market is packed with first-time home purchasers.

Currently, the mortgage industry is quite competitive; therefore, you shouldn't settle for anything but the best interest rates. There are various types of mortgages that are available, and your primary aim should be to find the one that best suits your needs.

Once you're able to decide on the type of mortgage (whether a fixed rate or an adjustable rate mortgage) that is most suitable for you, you can start shopping for the best interest rates. Interest rates are known to fluctuate on a regular basis; therefore, you should begin your search by tracking the present interest rates.

Your neighborhood is an excellent place to start shopping around for mortgage interest rates, particularly your local credit union or bank. These lenders have a history of offering their existent customers some of the most competitive mortgage loan interest rates.

You also have the option of using a mortgage broker. As mentioned earlier, a mortgage broker acts as a go-between for you and the lending company. As a result, the mortgage broker has access to interest rates offered by various lending companies, and can easily compare the rates and provide you with the best one.

Another way in which you can compare the mortgage interest rates of several lending companies is by visiting websites that specialize in the comparison of mortgage interest rates. Some of these websites charge a small fee; however, you'll find several free services as well.

Not only do online mortgage lenders provide you with more competitive rates, but they also enable you to do a side-by-side comparison of the interest rates of some of the most popular lenders in a short period of time.

If a mortgage interest rate seems too good to be true, then it most likely is. Ensure that you review the mortgage costs and terms with a fine tooth comb. You should also be mindful of mortgage points and of the fact that various lenders use different names to apply to the same costs, so be careful and remember to ask questions.

Learn to Negotiate Mortgage Points

Once you start your research on mortgage loans, you'll surely come across the term mortgage points. In simple terms, these points are fees that are directly linked to the interest rate, and are paid to the lending company. Keep in mind that you can decrease the fixed interest rate of your mortgage by paying more points.

Generally, a single mortgage point is equivalent to one percent of the loan amount. For instance, $4,000 is a single mortgage point for a loan amount of $400,000 (i.e. 1% of $400,000 = $4,000).

Usually, you'll be required to pay your mortgage points in cash, at closing time. There are some homebuyers who borrow money to pay their points; however, this will only increase the loan amount and the closing costs.

Will purchasing mortgage points save you money in the long run? Truth be told, there'll only be a slight decrease in your interest rate when you purchase mortgage points. Normally, your interest rate is lowered by 0.125 percent per mortgage point. For instance, if your interest rate is 8.5 percent, it will be decreased to 8.375 percent when you purchase a single mortgage point.

A mortgage point calculator is the best tool to use to help you determine how much money you'll be able to save monthly. It can also aid in determining the length of time it will take you to arrive at the *"breakeven"* point.

You'll attain the breakeven point when you're able to redeem the cost of buying mortgage points. Calculating your breakeven point is done in four simple steps. These are:

1. Compute your monthly mortgage payment amount at the standard interest rate.

2. Compute your monthly mortgage payment amount as if you had bought a single mortgage point.

3. Subtract your number two answer (the lower payment) from your number one answer (the higher payment).

4. Divide a single mortgage point amount by your number three answer (the amount saved monthly). The result is the length of time (in months) it will take you to attain the breakeven point.

The best way for you to decide whether or not you should buy mortgage points is to determine if you'll be able to incur the cost of the upfront payment at closing time.

If you won't be able to make the payments for mortgage points, you should abstain from purchasing them. Additionally, refrain from borrowing to purchase mortgage points, because (as mentioned earlier) this will only increase your loan amount and the closing costs.

When deciding whether or not to buy mortgage points, you need to take into consideration the length of time for which you plan to keep the mortgage. It's better to purchase mortgage points for a longer term mortgage than a shorter term one, as you'll benefit more from paying a reduced interest rate over a longer period of time.

It's advised that prior to signing for the loan, you negotiate the mortgage points. Before you go and see your mortgage broker or lender, research the current rates of the mortgage industry so that you'll have a better understanding of the expected cost of purchasing mortgage points.

There's also the option of having the seller pay for a fraction of the mortgage points. However, you first need to discuss this with your mortgage lender or broker to see if this option is available.

If the option is indeed available, you can go ahead and negotiate with the lender or broker to see what fraction of the mortgage points they are willing to pay.

Are you certain about purchasing mortgage points? If you are, then you should ask your lender or broker to quote the points as a dollar amount instead of as a percentage.

This will enable you to know the exact amount that you'll need to pay. You'll also find it easier to negotiate when you're working with the dollar amount rather than with the percentage.

Going Through Mortgage Paperwork with a Fine Tooth Comb

Filling out paperwork can be tedious and time-consuming at times, and it will make you wonder about the importance of including such detailed information on your application.

You ought to keep in mind that purchasing a home is one of the biggest decisions you'll ever make; as such, it's imperative that you take time out to accurately complete the application. Furthermore, discrepancies on your application will result in the extension of the application process, or your loan being denied.

Although there are various types of lending institutions on the market today, they all have a standard residential loan application form that you'll be required to fill out. The information required is generally broken down into eight categories. These are:

1. **Mortgage Type and Terms** – Here is where you'll select the mortgage type that you're applying for. This section also contains information such as the length of the loan, the interest rate, and the borrowed amount.

2. **Purpose of Loan and Property Information** – In this section, you'll be required to cite the purpose of the loan, and also state what type of property you're interested in purchasing. The lender needs to know if your loan is for refinancing, construction, or to purchase a property that's already built.

3. **Co-Borrower and Borrower Information** – You'll be required to fill out personal information such as your previous and present addresses. This information is also required for the co-borrower.

4. **Employment Information** – It's very important that you accurately list your employment information on your application, as the lending company needs to know that you are and will continue to be in a financial situation that will enable you to repay the loan.

The information generally required in this section is your monthly income, length of time you've been working in the profession and at your current job and your employer's contact information. If you have more than one job, ensure that you include the employment information for all jobs. Your co-borrower will need to fill out this section as well.

5. **Monthly Expenses and Income** – The lending company requires a detailed synopsis of how much money you're earning and spending on a monthly basis. For your monthly income, you'll need to include information relating to your base pay, commissions, interest credits and overtime. As for your expenses, include information like your monthly insurance costs and taxes.

6. **Liabilities and Assets** – In this section you should add the account number, contact information and name of anyone to whom you owe money. Additionally, you should include information regarding all the bonds, stocks and accounts you have.

7. **Transaction Details** – Here is where all the costs relating to the purchase of your home are listed. These costs include purchase price, repairs or alterations costs, as well as closing costs.

8. **Declaration** – In this section, you'll be required to check "*yes*" or "*no*" beside certain facts about your personal life. By signing the application form, you're guaranteeing that all the information provided is correct; as such, you should ensure that you answer all questions truthfully. Questions asked will be related to: lawsuit involvements, child support payments, alimony payments and bankruptcy.

Lying on your application will result in your loan being denied.

There are a few other details that you need to be aware of when filling out your application form. Ensure that the contact information of yourself, your co-borrower and your employer are all up-to-date. Additionally, you need to ensure that you sign everywhere your signature is required. Bear in mind that you may be asked to initial certain pages.

It's always good to have two copies of the residential loan application form. You can practice on one, and use the other one to enter your mistake-free information.

Remember that you're never alone in the loan application process. If you're not certain about something or have questions about the type of information that should be filled in on the application, don't hesitate to talk to your lending company, mortgage broker, or real estate agent.

Closing Costs and Fees Need-to-Knows

When you take out a mortgage loan, you must keep in mind that closing costs can total a huge amount. This is why it's very important for you to obtain a GFE (Good Faith Estimate) from your broker or lender, prior to you applying for the loan.

Having an idea of all the fees and closing costs that will be applied, will allow you to be more prepared for paying the closing costs when the time comes.

Items that are included in the closing costs are:

- Reserves collected by the lender for future insurance and taxes.

- Title Insurance

- Homeowner's Insurance

- Prepaid Interest

- Credit Reports

- Appraisals

- Attorney Fees

- Real Estate Transactions

  Every one of these items will add up, once you've made all the necessary payments towards your mortgage loan. Generally, estimated closing costs fall between $3,000 and $4,000.

  However, this is dependent on the various types of documentation, insurance and inspections that need to be attended to prior to you being able to call the house your very own. Here's a look at some of the fees that you'll be expected to pay at closing time.

- **Appraisal Fee** – This is one of the first fees that will be applied to your closing costs. An appraisal is an estimate of the true value of your home at closing time. It also includes information about what the best use of your property will be. Depending on the real estate value (at that particular time) and the area in which you reside, you should expect to pay between $200 and $450 for your appraisal fee.

- **Commitment Fee** – Lenders will charge you a commitment fee for an undisbursed loan or unused credit line. Generally, this fee is a fixed percentage of the amount of the undisbursed loan.

- **Application Fee** – This is fee is obviously for the mortgage loan application, and is paid at closing time.

- **Attorney Fees** – At the closing time of your loan, attorneys are used to review all the documentation that applies to the closing costs. This fee is their payment for reviewing the documentation.

- **Broker Fees** – If you employed the services of a broker, be prepared to pay him a fee for all the processing and administrative duties he performed.

- **Document Preparation Fee** – If another third party prepared your loan closing documents other than your broker, you're going to be required to pay a fee for this. Loan closing documents include: Power of Attorney; Release of Trust; Housing Authority Addendum; Warranty Deed; and Deed of Trust.

- **Closing Fee** – There will be some instances when a closing fee will be required, particularly in cases where a third party (e.g. a real estate agent) aids in closing the deal.

Apart from the fees listed above, other costs that you'll incur at loan closing time are related to inspection and insurance. Popular closing cost insurances include:

- **Homeowners Insurance** – You're required to obtain this type of insurance at least a year in advance, as a means of protecting your home and all the assets that you have inside your home.

- **Title Insurance** – This particular type of insurance ensures that the property title is free of defects. In other words, it provides protection against any loss from errors in the property title.

- **Flood Insurance** – At closing time, you'll be asked to pay flood insurance only if you're residing in a flood zone. It's also possible for you to get a flood certification. By paying the flood insurance, you'll be able to have flood zone status while repaying your mortgage loan, and even after the mortgage has been repaid.

- **Hazard Insurance Premium** – This particular type of insurance guarantees protection against specific types of risks like fires or storms.

The inspection fees which will be required at closing time include:

- **Home Inspection Fee** – This generally costs about $300.

- **Pest Inspection Fee** – This is to ensure that your home is pest-free.

- **Well and Septic Inspection Fee** – The condition of your home's well and septic tank will be assessed.

Assessments and property taxes are also costs that will be added to your closing costs. The most popular mortgage tax deposit is the escrow. Another type of tax that will be applied to your closing costs is the transfer tax.

In regards to closing your mortgage, you must always strive to find the most reasonable fees and the best way to obtain the necessary documentation. Keep in mind that there are free mortgage tools that will provide you with a quote of your closing costs.

Advantages and Disadvantages of Balloon Payment Mortgages

Although you were introduced to balloon payments earlier in this guide, there are still some things that you need to take into consideration prior to selecting this type of mortgage payment.

Just to refresh your memory, a balloon payment is a type of mortgage repayment plan, which allows you to pay a lump sum at the end of a period of smaller payments.

Persons normally opt for balloon payment mortgages when they are expecting a type of dividend, a huge tax refund, inherited money, or when they are refinancing their home.

Balloon payments won't be the best option for everyone; however, if you're considering this type of mortgage, you should get acquainted with some of the advantages and disadvantages of balloon payments.

Advantages:

- Down payments for balloon payment mortgages are generally lower than that of other types of mortgages.

- Lower interest payments are normally associated with balloon payments, which will result in a small capital outlay. Choosing this type of mortgage will enable you to have more adaptability in advancing the capital during the loan.

- Monthly payments for balloon payment mortgages are typically lower than the monthly payments for other types of mortgages.

- Interest rates of balloon payments won't change when the national rates increase. Once the rate is set at the start of the loan, it will remain the same throughout the loan period.

Keep in mind that if your expected money (that you plan on using to make the balloon payment) doesn't come through, you may be able to change your lump sum payment to smaller ones at any period of the loan. However, prior to signing the contract for a balloon payment mortgage, ensure that this option is available to you.

Disadvantages:

- The payment required at closing will be rather large. If you're unsure whether or not you'll have the money at a certain time, then it would be best to make an investment.

- In the end, the refinancing cost may turn out to be more than you expected. If while you're in a balloon payment the interest rates increase, you'll find yourself paying extra costs at closing time.

Remember that if the rates increase to more than five percent of the balloon interest rate with which you started, not only will you have to re-qualify for the loan but a reappraisal of your home will be required as well.

There are certain factors that you must take into consideration prior to getting a balloon payment mortgage. These are inclusive of:

- The starting interest rate.

- The time which the balance owed should be paid.

- Available refinance options.

- If it will be possible for you to switch from a balloon payment to a regular payment.

- Whether or not you'll be required to re-qualify for a mortgage loan once the last payments are due.

Once you have chosen a balloon payment mortgage, it's imperative that you keep in mind that you'll be able to acquire the fixed amount by the due date of the final balance.

It's also imperative that you consider what will transpire after you have paid the due payment, as you don't want to get stuck in a never-ending cycle of borrowing loans for your home.

If you have properly compared the advantages and disadvantages of a balloon payment mortgage and are confident that you'll have the end money when it's due, then you can go ahead and apply for this loan. On the other hand, if you won't be able to pay the lump sum, you should consider applying for another type of mortgage.

What Are Bridge Loans?

Are you interested in purchasing a house but are unable to secure permanent financing? If you're in this position, a bridge loan will be the most suitable solution to your problem.

A bridge loan (also referred to as *"gap financing"* or *"swing loan"*) is a type of short-term loan that provides you with quick cash until you're able to secure permanent financing. You're expected to repay the loan quickly, as the term for a bridge loan is generally between six months and a year.

A great percentage of persons who take advantage of bridge loans are those potential homebuyers who haven't sold their present home, but are ready to make a new purchase.

When the residential real estate market is at its best and houses are sold as soon as they are listed, a bridge loan is essentially unnecessary. However, this loan is quite beneficial when the market is moving slowly.

Take a look at this scenario. You've finally found your dream home and you want to go ahead and purchase it; however, you can't move forward because your current home hasn't been sold as yet.

Taking advantage of a bridge loan will enable you to move forward with the process of purchasing your dream home. With a bridge loan, you'll be able to make your dream home's down payment, or you'll be able to pay off your current home's mortgage.

As with other types of loans available, there are different varieties of the bridge loan. One of the more popular types of bridge loans are those that give you enough money to pay off your current home's mortgage.

A Typical Bridge Loan Works as Follows:

You're given enough money to pay off your current home's mortgage, as well as to make a down payment on your dream home. Typically, six months of prepaid interest and closing costs are deducted from the amount of the loan.

After the six-month term if your house is still not sold, you'll be allowed to start paying interest-only payments. Once your home is sold, you can pay off the entire bridge loan with unearned interest payments that were credited to you.

However, it's very important that you're aware of the fact that it may cost you a lot if you choose to use the bridge loan as it's used in the scenario above. Keep in mind that very high fees are often times applied to bridge loans; therefore, you must ensure that you comprehend all the terms and conditions prior to signing off on the loan.

Additionally, the possibility of you paying the equal amount of three mortgage payments (the actual loan amount, the new house and the present house) exists, until your current home is sold.

Before you make the leap and sign off on a bridge loan, have a talk with your real estate agent and find out all you can about the condition of the market. If the residential real estate market is moving rather slowly, it would be unwise for you to sign off on a bridge loan.

Frequently, bridge loans are utilized in real estate investing. If you have an interest in investing in real estate but are unable to access traditional loans, you can make your purchase using a bridge loan.

You'll find that a fair percentage of persons who use bridge loans are those who can't qualify for a traditional loan because of a bad credit score. As such, a majority of bridge loans offered via non-conventional lenders offer interest rates that fall between 14 and 20 percent.

These non-conventional lenders also allow persons to use mortgage points on bridge loans. These loans are far more accessible, as the lenders aren't as concerned with credit scores as conventional lenders are; however, bridge loans can be very expensive.

Bridge loans provide you with a quick and easy way to get cash infusion; per contra, their interest rates and average fees are a lot higher than conventional loans. The most important thing that you can remember about these loans is: *"don't apply for one if you don't need it."*

What Does Home Refinancing Entail?

Over the past few years, based on the condition of the real estate market, there have been quite a number of homeowners who have made the bold decision to refinance the mortgage on their home.

Refinancing your home can be beneficial, as it results in lower interest rates and mortgage monthly payments, which will enable you to save or spend more of your income on other expenses.

Home refinancing isn't for everyone. With that being said, you should ensure that this option is the most suitable option for you prior to you starting the application process. Listed below is some important information about refinancing that you must take into consideration.

- **Should You Take the Step to Refinance?** – Your interest rates will pay an integral part in your decision to refinance. It's worth refinancing your present mortgage if the new interest rate you'll have to pay is more than ½ percent to ⅝ percent of your present interest rate. If you wish for your closing costs to be as low as you can possibly get them, your present rate needs to be at least one percent lower.

- **How Much Can Be Saved With Refinancing?** – The amount you save with refinancing is based on a varied number of factors. For instance, you can save a reasonable amount of money when your interest rates are very low. Additionally, you can save quite a lot when your rates increase, and you refinance from a conventional loan to a flexible rate loan.

- **Refinancing Benefits** – Before you refinance your home, you need to consider all the advantages that apply. If you should ask someone who has refinanced his home before about the number one benefit of home refinancing, he'll probably tell you that it's saving money. However, other than saving money, other refinancing benefits exist. These are inclusive of:

    - <u>Lowering Monthly Loan Installments</u> – If you're able to lower your monthly loan installments, you can refinance your current mortgage at a lower interest rate.

    - <u>Consolidating Debts</u> – You can opt for refinancing as a means of consolidating your debts. By doing this, you'll be able to replace all your high-interest rate debts with a single low-interest monthly payment.

- <u>Additional Tax Deductions</u> – Decreased interest rates signify lesser interest deductions on Schedule A.

- <u>Mortgage Interest</u> – You're permitted to subtract interest on a debt maximum of one million dollars acquired to purchase your home and an additional one.

- <u>Points</u> – Refinancing allows you to use points, which are prepaid interests that need to be subtracted during the mortgage term, unless you have made improvements to your current primary property.

Shopping for the Best Second Mortgage Terms

If you're shopping around for a second mortgage, ensure that you spend quality time searching for the best deals that are most suitable for the needs of your family.

There are several reasons homeowners look for second mortgages. These reasons may include:

- Looking for a faster way to repay the first mortgage.

- Increase equity.

- Consolidate debts.

- Decrease monthly payments

No matter your reason for seeking a second mortgage, there are a few factors that you must first take into consideration before signing off on that second mortgage. Here are some of those factors to consider.

- **Qualified Lenders** – You'll find lenders in various locations such as credit unions, mortgage companies, commercial banks and thrift institutions. Each of these lenders has different terms and prices that you need to carefully consider. You also have the choice of using a mortgage broker; however, if you use a mortgage broker, be sure to choose the one that will provide you with the best options.

- **Pricing** – As mentioned earlier, you need to bear in mind that there are a variety of prices that apply to mortgages (second mortgages as well). With that being said, you need to strive to get the best prices on:

    - <u>Interest Rates</u> – These rates can be adjustable or fixed.

    - <u>Annual Percentage Rate (APR)</u> – This includes: credit charges, broker fees and interest rates.

    - <u>Fees Included in the Loan Amount</u> – This includes: settlement fees, broker fees, closing costs, transaction fees and underwriting fees. You have the option of paying these fees in a lump sum. Ensure that you get the individual costs of these fees, as well as the sum of all of them.

- ▪ <u>Down Payment</u> – On average, the down payment is approximately 20 percent of the house's purchase price. Some lending companies and brokers will allow you to pay less. You also have the option of submitting a lesser down payment, by purchasing PMI (Private Mortgage Insurance). This particular type of insurance covers the lender if payments aren't received.

- **Bad Credit Score** – You can still obtain a second mortgage with a bad credit score; however, it will take some work, as you'll have to find the right lender that's going to cater to your situation.

- **Equal Credit Opportunity Act** – Based on this act, mortgage lenders cannot refuse to give you a mortgage because of your age, sex, ethnicity, sexual orientation, handicap, etc.

Shopping around for a second mortgage is quite similar to shopping for a first mortgage. However, you need to take into consideration your primary reason for taking out a second mortgage, shop around for the best deals, and then make your final decision.

Reasons Your Mortgage Loan Has Been Denied

You have filled out your mortgage loan application properly. You hand it in to the lending company and wait for the call that tells you that your loan has been granted. You finally get the call, only to be told that your loan has been denied.

Didn't you provide them with all the necessary documents? Didn't you provide them with accurate information? So, why was your loan denied? Here are a few of the most popular reasons mortgage companies deny loans.

- **The Property's Appraised Value is too Low** – In this case, your mortgage company calculated that the ratio of the amount of the loan to the sale price or to the property's appraised value was far lower than that of LTV (Loan-to-Value) or purchase price ratio. Or it could be that the LTV is much higher than the amount the mortgage company can approve. Additionally, if the loan amount you applied for falls between 90 and 95 percent of the purchase price, your loan will be denied.

If the seller's asking price far exceeds the rates in your area, you should go back to the drawing board and renegotiate the price with him. Try your best to work with a purchase price that the mortgage company wouldn't refuse. If you're unable to do so, the next best thing to do is to use your personal funds to pay the balance, and apply for a smaller loan amount.

- **Insufficient Funds** – Another reason that may cause your mortgage loan to be denied is a lack of funds. This generally happens when the lender has gone through your financial records and notice that you don't have sufficient funds for the down payment or closing costs.

  Insufficient funds also refer to a low income. If your mortgage payment is going to surpass 28 percent of your gross monthly income, your loan will most likely be denied. Keep in mind though that FHA loans generally have a higher number. On the other hand, if you have a great credit card record and can also prove that you have quite a lot of household expenses, the mortgage lender may these things into consideration.

- **Too Much Debt** – Typically, your mortgage loan application won't be denied solely because of your debt amount. However, if you have a number of account balances that are very close to the prescribed limit or credit cards that constantly get maxed out, then you may be denied the loan. Additionally, your loan can be denied if your total debt surpasses 36 percent of your gross monthly income. Prior to reapplying for your mortgage loan, ensure that you repay as many of your debts as possible.

- **Bad Credit History** – This was talked about earlier. If you have a history of missing or making late payments, the mortgage lender most likely won't approve you for a mortgage loan. A lending company wants to be sure that you'll repay the loan, and if you have a history of not repaying your debts then the company will not want to do business with you. As such, you must always try to repay your debts on time, and avoid missing payments.

Yes, you've been denied a mortgage loan; however, that doesn't mean that your life is over. There are always corrective measures that you can take to improve your loan acceptance chances. First, you must find out the exact reason for your loan being denied, and tackle that problem so that you won't be denied again when you reapply.

Should You Repay Your Mortgage Loan Early or Not?

There's one question that continues to gnaw at the back of the minds of most homeowners and that is, *"should you invest your money or repay your mortgage loan early?"* You'll get a varied number of answers to this question, and this only proves that one solution doesn't suit everyone.

Consider this. If you think of your additional mortgage payments as if they were an investment and the return as the loan's interest, you'll need to contemplate whether or not you'll be able to go elsewhere and get higher returns. If you can, go ahead and invest the money and keep your mortgage.

With that being said, keeping your mortgage or deciding to pay it off shouldn't be a decision that you rush into. There are multiple factors that will influence your decision, including whether or not you want to deal with a huge loan, your current cash-flow and your tax bracket. You'll have to consider the present financial situation in your life, prior to making this decision.

For example, if your career is at its peak, don't rush to do an early mortgage repayment. Take into consideration that if your income is high, your income tax will be high as well. However, the good news is that the interest on your mortgage is another income tax deduction you can claim.

Additionally, you can benefit from the deduction of your mortgage interest if you opt to repay a larger percentage of your interest earlier in the loan term. This can be accomplished by paying additional installments throughout the year.

If you have a low mortgage rate, think about investing your money in financial schemes that will offer you greater returns. However, if your mortgage rates are on the higher end of the spectrum, invest your money in your home as this warrants you higher rates of interest.

For instance, if you have a 16 percent mortgage, you can acquire a 16 percent rate of interest if you repay it early. In no time at all, you'll be mortgage-free.

If you're approaching retirement age, you'll most likely want to speed up your loan repayments so that you'll be debt-free when you finally stop working. If you plan on taking this step, you need to ensure that repaying your mortgage loan early doesn't become a burden.

Take a Look at the Following Scenario:

You make the decision to refinance your mortgage in order to lessen your loan term to 15 years, and that by the age of 65 you'll have a nil balance. Because of this, rather than paying $750 monthly for your interest and principal payment, it will increase to $950 monthly. When pay-off day arrives, you can invest the $950 in a fund that will guarantee you a nine percent interest. In another 15 years, you'll have a total of $360,000.

On the other hand, if you're already retired, you may notice that you're repaying more principal than you are mortgage interest. If this is the case, your primary focus will be on completely repaying your mortgage loan, and you may also experience problems with cash-flow.

If you're aware that after you retire you'll be experiencing problems with cash-flow, the best thing to do is to repay your mortgage loan early. However, if you have no assets or just a few, it would be wise for you to expand your investments.

For instance, you should think about opening a money market or savings account, which would provide you with greater returns than what you're paying for your mortgage interest.

If you have recently finalized a sale on a huge house and are loaded with cash, it would be best to take out a mortgage, but only if your investment returns will be greater than your mortgage interest.

When you don't tie up all your available cash in the real estate market, you can benefit from tax deduction, invest in a variety of financial schemes and have more liquidity at hand. Your mortgage loan won't only be repaid in full, but you'll never have to worry about it when you retire.

The Fundamentals of PMI (Private Mortgage Insurance)

Private Mortgage Insurance or PMI is a type of insurance that you'll need to buy if your down payment is low. As such, if your down payment is 20 percent or less of the appraised value of the property or the sale price, you should purchase PMI.

Private mortgage insurers are responsible for creating this product, and it's designed to protect lenders in the event that home purchasers default on their loan.

PMI has aided millions of people (particularly first-time homeowners), as it enables individuals to purchase homes with lesser down payments than what was previously accepted. As the prices of homes continue to reach an all-time high, it has become quite imperative to buy homes with a lesser down payment.

Additionally, PMI aids prospective homeowners to purchase their dream homes a lot sooner, as now many persons can get a home with a down payment as low as five percent. Furthermore, a PMI can assist you in qualifying for several other home loans.

You'll find that PMI costs vary based on the mortgage loan and the down payment; however, it's generally equivalent to a half of one percent of the loan total. Having said that, how is Private Mortgage Insurance computed?

Let's say you purchased a home for $100,000 with a down payment of 10 percent. The remaining 90 percent is multiplied by 0.005 percent, and the result ($450 in this case) will be your annual PMI. This amount will then be subdivided into monthly payments.

Some years after you have been repaying your mortgage loan, you should be able to quit paying PMI. Remember to always keep record of your payments so that when you attain 80 percent equity, you can contact your mortgage lender and have them cancel your PMI.

The Homeowner's Protection Act was passed in 1999, and requires all lenders to inform buyers of the exact number of months and years it will take for them to repay the 20 percent of their principal. Although this act is in place, it's still advised that you keep your own records.

The Homeowner's Protection Act also gives lenders the power to make specific buyers continue paying PMI up to 50 percent equity. However, this only applies to those buyers who are considered to be *"high risk borrowers."* There are even some FHA (Federal Housing Administration) loans that demand that home purchasers get PMI for the entirety of the mortgage loan.

If you detest the idea of having to pay PMI for years, you should know that there are now ways for you to avoid paying this insurance, even when you're unable to pay the 20 percent down payment.

One strategy used to avoid paying PMI is to pay more interest on the mortgage loan. There are some mortgage companies that will relinquish the requirement for PMI if you agree to pay more interest on your mortgage loan. A benefit of using this strategy is that your mortgage interest will become tax deductible.

Another strategy utilized to avoid paying PMI is the *"80-10-10"* loan strategy. This involves having two loans and paying a 10 percent down payment on your new home.

One loan will aid in financing 80 percent of your mortgage, while the other will aid in financing 10 percent of the sale price. The second mortgage that covers the 10 percent of the sale price generally has higher interest rates.

However, since the loan amount is low, it's quite easy to repay the interest rates. Under the 80-10-10 loan strategy, the mortgage interest is tax deductible as well.

Yet another way in which you can cancel your PMI is if you can prove that the value of your home has significantly increased. If your home's value has increased, then you have most likely already paid 20 percent or more of the equity that's needed to end PMI payments.

You'll need to submit evidence of the increase in the value of your home to the mortgage lender; however, the process is quite slow. Be prepared to wait for a period of two years for the mortgage lender to make a final decision.

If you're required to pay PMI for a longer period or up until the end of the term of the loan, this may be a result of your poor credit history. If you find yourself in this position, you should talk to your mortgage lender about how changes in your credit record will have an effect on paying for PMI.

Is Home Equity Refinancing Right for You?

Today, home equity financing has become a practicable option for a lot of homeowners, as during the last decade the real estate market has consistently been doing well. As a result, this has made the option of loan or credit home equity financing worth considering.

Even though the prices of homes continue to increase, many persons still consider purchasing a home to be a smart investment. This shows that regardless of the economic outlook, your home's value continues to appreciate. This should probably give you the push you need to start considering taking out a line of credit or a home equity loan.

- **Why Should You Consider Home Equity Financing?** – Two concrete reasons for you to consider home equity financing are the boost in the real estate market and the increasing value of your home.

Home equity financing also comes with several tax advantages. In fact, you may be able to lower your taxes by claiming the interest paid on your home equity credit. Keep in mind that home equity products carry lower interest rates and thus lower monthly payments.

- **How to Get the Best Out of Home Equity Refinancing?** – Using a home equity loan to repay high interest loans and refinance your debt, is one way in which you can get the best out of home equity refinancing. However, if you're debt-free, you can choose instead to increase the value of your home by improving it.

- **What's the Right Type of Home Equity Plan for Your Needs?** – Based on your needs, you have the option of selecting a home equity credit line or a home equity loan. If you're able to estimate how much refinancing you'll need, a home equity loan will be the best option.

On the other hand, a home equity line of credit is more ideal if you cannot estimate how much refinancing you'll need, and if you're in need of money to help repay debts and lower your credit card balance.

Deciding to finance your home is a very important decision. It's true that several home equity products are available for you to choose from; however, your product selection should primarily be based on your current financial situation and goals.

We Want Your Feedback on This Book!

Our main purpose is to make sure that our readers get value from the books we publish and that they have a good experience with all of our products. We are always working to improve our books and other products with every revision and update.

Every piece of feedback makes a difference in this process. And we would appreciate yours as well - whether it is good or bad.

Please take one minute to let us know what you thought by following this link:

http://checkmatemg.com/feedbackmortgages/

www.ingramcontent.com/pod-product-compliance
Lightning Source LLC
Chambersburg PA
CBHW071800170526
45167CB00003B/1109